~More praise for *Lowering the Body*~

Following *The Oswego Fugues* and *Communion of Asiago*, Stephen Murabito consummates his trilogy for a former time and place: the 1960s and the West Eighth Street neighborhood of Oswego, New York, where people still carry the strong scents and accents of old countries. These lovely narrative poems—inflected with the "home ache" that is nostalgia's English translation—lament the loss of the local everywhere. As testament and elegy, they demonstrate the wages of trading "bad cheddar for good Gargonzola," but by writing, Murabito redeems even that defeat.

JULIA SPICHER KASDORF
MFA Program Director, Penn State University
Author of *Eve's Striptease*

Stephen Murabito's new collection, *Lowering the Body*, vividly brings to life a time, the 1960s, and place, upstate New York, that is lost to history, but beautifully rendered in these poems. As seen through the eyes of a child-observer whose Italian-American father runs one of those corner grocery stores that began disappearing by the end of that decade, the lives of an extended family, friends, and colorful neighbors are lovingly detailed. One hilarious and trenchant poem, "My Mother Joins the Hippies," portrays a moment in the community when protest of the Viet Nam War and women's rights accidentally met in the rural north: "Mrs. Berlin, Mrs. Ferraro, and Mrs. Grimaldi joined the hippies" protesting that a pregnant teacher who is "showing" has lost her job, Mother among the women joining the march and "Carrying the grocery stamper higher and higher like some kind of baton." In the heartbreaking "Burying Cousin Peter," the grieving father of the soldier son who died in Viet Nam beats "a man up onto his front porch/ . . . leaving him to bleed/ Into the last green of that year's tomatoes" and then gives his son's Cadillac to the man by way of apology. One thinks of today's lost sons and daughters, to which this poem relates. Murabito has a fine ear for spoken language, and an impeccable sense of the quotidian and the moral. This tender portrait of a backwater town registering on a daily level the impact of the great social changes of the 1960s is rich with narrative insight and at times ribald, life-affirming, Felliniesque humor.

CYNTHIA HOGUE
Author of *The Incognito Body* and *Flux*

*Lowering the Body*

*Lowering the Body*

STEPHEN MURABITO

*Lowering the Body*

Copyright © 2008
by Stephen Murabito

cover design by Trisha Hadley
cover photographs by Michael Murabito

*All rights reserved. No part of this book may be used or reproduced in any manner whatsoever without written permission from the publisher, except in the case of brief quotations embodied in articles and reviews.*

Published by

~Star Cloud Press®~
6137 East Mescal Street
Scottsdale, Arizona 85254-5418

ISBN:
978-1-932842-30-2 — $12.95

Library of Congress Control Number: 2008920150

Printed in the United States of America

OTHER BOOKS BY STEPHEN MURABITO

*Connections, Contexts, and Possibilities*, Prentice Hall, 2001
[a composition reader]

*A Little Dinner Music*, Parallel Press, 2004

*The Oswego Fugues*, Star Cloud Press, 2005

*Communion of Asiago*, Star Cloud Press, 2006

*Acknowledgments*

I am grateful to the editors of the following publications, where these poems first appeared, some in slightly different forms: "First Prophecy" and "The Family Way," *Pittsburgh Quarterly On-Line*; "Differing Versions," *Yalobusha Review*; "Eating Pepperoni on Good Friday," *North American Review*; "Delivering Sfogliatelle to Cousin May," *Poet Lore*; "This Is My Ode," *5AM*; "A White Baldness," *Pittsburgh City Paper*; "Vittorio and Conchetina," *Loyalhanna Review*; "Four Quarts, Four Loaves" and "Parents Sleeping," *Fourth River On-Line*; "My Mother's Goose-Stepping Rage," *Colere*; "Saby Closes the Store, January, 1969," *Italian-Americana*.

"Eating Pepperoni on Good Friday" also appears in *Encore: More of Parallel Press Poets*, edited by Elisabeth R. Owens (Parallel Press, 2006).

"In Love with the B-Girls" and "Blessings, Cursings: The Chained Shelves" also appear in *Along These Rivers*, edited by Judith R. Robinson and Michael Wurster (Quadrant Publishing, 2008).

*For my family,*
*for our corner store,*
*for 159 West Eighth Street,*
*for the life left there.*

# Contents

| | |
|---|---|
| First Prophecy, 1962 | 1 |
| Differing Versions | 3 |
| Eating Pepperoni on Good Friday | 5 |
| Fritz Rosczinski: Refrigerator Repairman | 6 |
| Kelly Stanelli | 8 |
| Delivering Sfogliatelle to Cousin May | 13 |
| This Is My Ode | 15 |
| Four Quarts, Four Loaves | 18 |
| Parents Sleeping | 20 |
| The Mass Card Lady | 21 |
| Stealing My Father's Shoes | 24 |
| Father's Day, Fair Haven Beach, 1966 | 26 |
| Home Run, MacArthur Stadium, Syracuse, New York | 28 |
| A White Baldness | 29 |
| The Confetti | 30 |
| Aunt Dee | 32 |
| Burying Cousin Peter | 34 |
| The Family Way | 37 |

| | |
|---|---|
| Lowering the Body | 41 |
| Vittorio and Conchetina | 42 |
| Your Knives | 43 |
| Kahn the Great | 46 |
| My Mother Joins the Hippies | 48 |
| My Mother's Goose-Stepping Rage | 51 |
| In Love with the B-Girls | 54 |
| Blessings, Cursings: The Chained Shelves | 55 |
| | |
| Coda: Saby Closes the Store, January, 1969 | 59 |
| | |
| About the Author | 61 |

What can I do with this longing for that union,
Touching their faces, then my own.
      Patricia Dobler
        "Two Photographs"

# Lowering the Body:
# The West Eighth Street Sequence

First Prophecy, 1962

Once upon a time,
On the corner of West Eighth and Oneida,
A six year-old boy
Stood up on a coffee table,
Kicked aside issues of *Look* and *Life*,
And shouted, *Giants, Giants, Giants!*
The gathered Sunday clan
Of die-hard Yankee fans
Paused, stunned in salted Planters and cold Genesee.
In the flashing Sylvania background,
Mantle rounded third into eternity.
But the boy, passionate as Perry Mason,
Shouted, *Mays, McCovey, Alou, Marichal, Cepeda!*
And for ten detonating seconds,
He stood on *Reader's Digest* and *Time*,
Stood in brown-eyed love and passion,
In olive-skinned loyalty and conviction,
In short-sleeved righteousness and vision.
He knew this first prophecy scared
The pinstriped hell out of them.
Yes, in seconds of shallow breath,
Their eyes asked, *Who is this anomaly,*
*This false prophet, this brazen free thinker?*
*Who is this damned National League fan?*

And life began again
As he was swept away to Wise chips and a Coke
By the chattering Sicilian grandmother,
Who was the only one not to laugh,
Who was the only one to whisper, *He'sa touched,*
Who was the only one to lower her head into,
*Santa Lucia, Santa Teresa, Santa Maria . . .*
As Roger Maris tapped the dirt,
Shrugged his shoulders,
Held that bat high,
Smiled into death,
And dug in at the plate.

Differing Versions

The hellish black cloud drew breath
Over our corner grocery.
This was 1963.

Eighth Street still tells it today,
How the boy climbed to the top
Of the blue '50 Buick—

Broad-shouldered delivery car—
And howled up to the black sky,
*No! No! No! This place is ours!*

*You cannot wash it away!*
Customers gathered outside
And laughed until Grandma Z

Knelt with bread and cured olives,
Turning to Sicilian chants
As the sun burst over him,

Setting rusted chrome ablaze.
Those left say he spoke in tongues,
Stilling thunder with such blood.

Some say the clouds parted when
His arms dropped into silence.
Some say his hands were wingtips

As he flew down the back hood
To disappear up Eighth Street.
But one insists he stayed there,

Head lifting into his life.
Either way, they all agree:
That two-toned Special shimmered

And burnt to the touch for days.

# Eating Pepperoni on Good Friday
*-for my son, Sebastian-*

After stealing the magic stick from my father's meat case,
I try to think of where to go. Not into the closet off the kitchen,
Where the smell will hang with that of salty boots; not down

To the cellar with webs on my face, or out back to the '50 Buick.
I must go where only my punishment can follow: I go up to the roof,
High over Eighth Street. Only God, above the oaks, can spot me,

The weight of my sin hard in my hands. Oh, it's terrible, I know,
To eat Pastucci Brothers' on Good Friday, everyone in dark rooms,
The thin bible pages turning slowly to the Sorrowful Mysteries.

And I'm caught as the chimney stack hisses red with anger.
Okay, okay, I accept it: I will pick each sandy grain
From every last rooftop on Eighth Street; I will be sentenced

To an eternity of shingles, standing here forever, veils of steam
From Friday flounder rising without me. Yes, but first, this bite,
Teeth breaking salty skin, smell drifting straight up to Heaven.

## Fritz Rosczinski: Refrigerator Repairman

Some connection in the store went haywire,
And Fritz Rosczinski appeared
Out of the sweet, salami-blessed air
To fix a fuse or mend a compressor
With a mumbled *shit-piss-fuck-damn*,
And exactly the right wrench or pair of pliers.

Johnny D, with the incense of a White Owl
And a pound of sausage tucked like a football,
Patted his joke on my head: *The crack
In Fritz's ass begins just south of Heaven.
Then it disappears under his tool belt
To plunge to the Gates of Hell.* They howled.

I had already seen the ghosts and specters
Wandering West Eighth and Oneida
Like miserable shoppers returning
Bad cheddar for good Gorgonzola.
I'd seen their tongues clicking to me,
*Your lives here are ticking away.*

So nothing terrified me more than
Fritz Rosczinski letting loose
The unimaginable gravity of that tool belt
And dismantling the store within minutes.
By the beer coolers, I told myself,
*Fritz Rosczinski is sent from God.*

Then the obscene angel who had moved in silence,
Even over the ancient center-aisle planks,
Was vaporized into the Campbell's soups.
Neither tool nor nut nor bolt was left behind.
I had slipped in my vigil by the Monks' bread:
I had lowered my head for just the seconds

It took to conquer the last of my Red Hot Dollars.

## Kelly Stanelli

*Presidents and rock stars come and go,*
*And that picture doesn't fade. It wasn't much,*
*But I stood there on the surface of the world*
*Feeling it as it made another turn.*

   Henry Taylor
   "An Instant on the Time Line"

### I

Marlboro butts and Labatt beer bottles,
Buzzy Seawell and three
Guys from the eastside
Tricked Kelly Stanelli to La Rock's Point,
Where water lay flat and still
Out to the horizon
Gone sunset maroon
To cobalt blue to black
Against the screams that the vacationers heard.

Across the inlet,
I fished with Billy Saint James,
His Newfoundland, Jasper, standing, sniffing,
His Uncle Willy asleep in the rusted Olds,
Three Gennies left to drown under spent ice.

Jasper lunged into the water,
The world reduced to a relentless black head
And the unstoppable breathing.

She made it to the beach,
And Jasper stood bellowing between her
And the four figures,
Who squealed away in Buzzy's '57 Bel Air.

Jasper turned to her, then to the inlet,
Then back to her:
He was the instinctive pronouncement,
*Come, I will take you*
*Across the dark water.*

II

That Sunday, Buzzy was at St. Joe's
For the 8:30 mass.
It was 1964. I was eight. I had a knife,
The dull, pointless thing
That Grandma Z worked to "Volare"
When she skinned sopressatta for us kids.

Behind Buzzy in communion line,
I poked the thick blade
Into his right thigh,
The tiny flap of white cotton spotting red.
I turned and stood
Before the stunned congregation,
The Virgin Mother
Freezing in her stained-glass Assumption,

Christ looking down
With the sadness of eternal comprehension.

**III**

Driving down brilliant First Street
To the police station,
Grandpa Z begged, *How comma you do that?*
*Who'sa he to you, huh?*
*If he do soma thing to you,*
*You tell me. You hear?*
Against Grandma Z's endless rosaries,
I said nothing,
Realizing for the first time
How words were a great music
But could never capture
Everything eyes saw,
And silence was more powerful—
At least on the leather back seat
Of that mammoth Chrysler Imperial.

He was squinting all the way back to Sicily:
*Well, at leasta you didn't kill him, huh?*
*Worse things happen ina this life.*
*You gonna live a long, long life.*

But I harnessed my expanding silence.

*Atsa okay. You keep quiet.*
*I say one, maybe two prayers, okay?*

And then began his chanting with her,
His husky mumbling of the Sacred Mysteries,
And I saw my name rise from their wet lips
And float out their windows.

He blessed himself, looked back at me,
And I wondered what *they* saw,
What *they* believed.

Oh, there we were, a caravan
Of panic, prayer, and pain:
My grandparents' faces turning
To hearts before God,
My parents' faces fast behind us now,
Lurching, lurching,
Up to the windshield
As if their bodies could propel the Pontiac faster.

Me and my *famiglia*—
Not a word to describe our
Slicing through the echo of madness,
Kelly's story to save me later,
But not one angel to bless us then,
Just engines hurling,
Just Oswego sky blue and burning,
Just the sun closing my mother's eyes
When her velvet hand
Led me from the car.

## Delivering Sfogliatelle to Cousin May

She lived down on the Railroad Flats,
Where soot and spit were tough enough
To still the Oswego River
At the hydroelectric plant:
The hum in deep green pools to black
Shot up through my sneaks to my heart
And was the God of Certainty.

The Erie Lackawanna tracks,
The grinding of its massive cars,
The brakes and horns of tractor trucks,
And the burning *Genny Beer* sign
From the black glass of Smitty's Bar:

Fear nailed my legs to the sidewalk
As I stopped on Pilsudski Street
And saw two hoods in pointed boots
Throw their fists until one boy fell,
The other's hands cutting his face.

The boy on the ground wailed through me,
*I give! I give! Leave me alone!*
But our cry was smashed into trains
And trucks and the canal's floodgates
Roaring the howl of earth itself.

How long had Cousin May been screaming
From her steps, then the road, for me
To run back home with the pastries?

But her shouting somehow calmed me
Into the alley where he lay,
And I gave him a sfogliatelle.
It crumbled in his shaking hands,
Red with blood and white with sugar:
*What? Who the fuck are you?* He moaned.

But I ran for my shouted name
And the hand that pulled me away.
She hugged the box like a child
And went inside to call the cops.

I stayed on her porch and waited:
He staggered out into the street,
Lunged and swayed his way down the hill,
Raised the sfogliatelle to his mouth,

And turned up river on First Street.

## This Is My Ode

We weren't allowed to let Uncle Ted into the kitchen,
Just give him a new Genny in the living room:
Oh, this is my ode to the sweet, foamy head of sixties
Psychotherapy. But no, a cook on early retirement,
He'd lose his balance, *go astray*, as Cousin May said.
Like when Ted cleaned fresh clams in the dishwasher:
Oh, this is my ode to all those sudsy yawners,
My ode to the perversion of soapy grinners,
My ode to that trigger inside us all, moved by what,
The mention of pastrami or a dead wife's name?

I saw it when he was behind the deli when the Fire Department
Ordered pastramis, and someone mentioned Aunt Peggy's name:
Oh, this is my ode to heaping mayo on corned beef
And my father storming out of his own store,
Bells howling at the door. Ted didn't even appear
To like this thing he'd made. He simply stood there
On the sawdust and regarded it at arm's length,
Eyes saying, *No, this isn't the peace I had thought.*
*But if I flee the world far enough . . .* Oh, hear me now,
This is my ode to a man setting down a sin of a sandwich
And calmly walking away, not a white hair out of place.

STEPHEN MURABITO

This is my ode to cold and entombed pain,
To Ted in the intersection of West First and Bridge,
The *Don't Walk* sign freezing him in his steps,
The world blowing its horns of forced stillness and outrage
At a man whose wife dropped dead at her ironing board,
And he said that over and over to the cops in their cruiser
As the people paused with their hands up to their mouths
Or their *Palladium Times* folded under their arms.

This is my ode to the biggest pastrami sandwiches
I've ever seen, gaping smilers with tongues hanging out
Like the tired runners we were that day, all the way
Downtown with our layers and layers and layers of meat,
Mustard, and cheese, and the Dortmunder pickles we'd fished out.
I carried the Campbell's Soup box into the station,
And we fed the cops, who said not to worry, just give him
A Genny and help him calm down, that they knew him
For years as the cook over at Vona's, how he and his wife
Shared a hot pastrami in the back booth on Friday nights.

Oh, this is my ode to the one cop's simple logic
With mustard on his chin and the rest of their happy mouths
Sinking into those monstrosities as we walked out and into
The blistering August afternoon of 1965, Ted like a child
Holding my hand, how such strange flesh engulfs your soul.

We got him back home, and my father turned at the door,
Looking cold and confused as he returned to his orders, his orders.
This is my ode to those eyes, those wordless eyes as I
Handed Ted the beer in the cool, doilied, brown-bottled darkness.
This is my ode to the way he took it, sipped it, then lowered
His head, to the way I looked at my mother and my Cousin May,
Who both stood looking from the dining room,
To the way the sun burst in through the latticed
Venetian blind, igniting their colorless work clothes,
Igniting their dark arms, igniting their paused,
Pondering faces, igniting for me, for the first time,
More than those resilient olive faces.

Four Quarts, Four Loaves
*~for my parents~*

> While Rochester received two feet of snow, the city of Oswego reported a total of approximately 100 inches.
>
> cnywinter.com

During the Blizzard of '66
The only thing that wasn't white
Was the inside of our house.
At last, after the two-hour trek

To get bread for his customers,
My father emerged from the front door,
Itself gone white around him.
He stood like a man who'd walked

From West Eighth and Oneida
To East Ninth and Bridge Street,
And back—a man who had pulled two sleds
Through every evil and beyond every winged beast.

But on the porch, there they were, dozens
Of loaves sitting upright like attentive children.
And I saw him, coming home on Bridge Street,
Pushing through step after step of his mission.

And I heard some music seeping
Through the wind—not a grand symphony,
But a simple folk song
About a man walking step on step.

After he thawed out,
He bagged the loaves with milk,
And he made a list of the older customers
Who *had* to have bread and milk that day.

My mother wrapped me in scarves of love
And fear. I had four trips to make:
Four quarts of milk, four loaves of bread.
They made me test the double-bagged weight

Of their concern before sending me
Into the sublime magic of simple mission,
My father's voice breaking through the white
Not to take a dime from anyone.

And I was gone, into the swirl of step
On step through the Oswego
Storm, where they must've known
That everything would break to me,

Even if it took years.

## Parents Sleeping

> *There are four primary forces holding the universe together:*
> *Gravity, magnetism, the strong force, and the weak force.*
>
> *Understanding Magnetism*, Part One
> The Discovery Channel

Oswego was buried. The store shut down.
We got up early to see the blizzard
Blacken the sky. We surged to radio
Cancellations, wolfing down our Corn Flakes.

I climbed the stairs up to my parents' room
And was held in the breath of my staring:
Who *were* these exhausted people, these dead
Beauties, the white covers muting their form?

What forces of life were holding them there,
The magnetism of their love, the strong
Force of their store, the weak force of fighting,
Or the gravity of their children, now,

One by one, bouncing them back to Eighth Street?

## The Mass Card Lady

I

She lived up Eighth Street, nearly to Bridge.
I was amazed that one person
Could know every church,
Every priest in Oswego,
All about the requiem masses,
The Office of the Dead,
And the Liturgy of the Hours.

I went up there for my mother
When Mrs. Luzinski died.
My mittens hung down,
Loaded with silver dollars.

My knees numb, I rang the door bell
Into another life,
The coins turning to stone,
No matter how hard I blew into my hands.

I stepped through their monastery doors
And died into the creaking floors
When her twisted shadow
Finally broke along the far wall.

II

No one knew how many days
He'd been in the basement,
Sitting with hammer and picture frame.
And she must've gotten so bad
That she never missed him,
Just went on rising, bathing,
Peeling potatoes, sitting above him,
And shaking salt over her plate.

No one knew how long
Until I went up there,
Strained on tiptoe
To steam a window,
Was let in, and smelled it
Pressing up into the trapped words
Of the old books, pressing up into
The kitchen's curling wallpaper.

III

My mother believed in child psychology,
So again, I sat on Dr. Day's couch
And was given inky shadows to interpret.

My father ranted, drank about it at Romero's,
Where Chubby Donnato said,
*Just get the kid boxing, Saby.*
*Christ, he's already built like a bull.*

But how could I tell them
All that I saw when that smell finished
Its pressing, pressing into me?
I saw him stare into the bent frame
As if waiting for the picture to return:
He broke through the flurries behind my eyes.
And that was exactly how they found him,
Back under the single bulb
Lit in the gray-stoned gravity
Of a man sitting on a rusted lawn chair.

And then one night,
Just when it seemed over,
My parents walked pane to pane
Across my bedroom window
On their way down Eighth to Romero's,
And I turned and saw her on my wall
Peeling potatoes at her sink
And thinking, *Yes, I'll go.*
But first the cutting, the salting, the boiling,
First, the day born of seconds
Giving birth to our lives.

And I saw a boy bounding up her steps.
He pressed the doorbell,
Squinting through the dark glass.
He peered beyond the trapped words,

Into the shadow-shift of his changing life.

### Stealing My Father's Shoes

Home sick on a Sunday morning,
The rest gone off to 10:00 mass,
I sneak down through the cellar
Up into my father's store,
To stand hidden by the paper goods,
The Ballantine Ale clock sweeping away
The seconds of the empty produce case.

I can stuff myself sicker with Twinkies
Or chocolate Sno balls dusted with coconut.
I can stuff my pockets with Hershey bars
Or the endless ticker-tape math of Necco Candy Buttons.

But instead, I go behind the white meat counter,
Look long into the wastebasket,
And see the shock of my father's shoes—
Wrinkled like an ancient face,
Torn at the eyelets, caked with ages
Of fallen meat and clinging sawdust,
Frayed down to the final rolled-roast,
Trimmed Porterhouse, or Sicilian sausage ring.

This is February 1966, and I can tell no one what I know
About the sweeping second hand above the battered phone
When the entire world is gone off to Saint Joe's,
And I am crouching low in this dark paradise.

I fly back home and hide
The cleaned shoes
Deep in my closet,
Back by my oiled glove,
The winter ball wrapped
Safely in its heart.

### Father's Day, Fair Haven Beach, 1966

Resplendent teenage girls saunter by,
WNDR from Syracuse riding on one's hip.

*Tinker to Evers to Chance,* my father says,
Taking snap after harder snap of the balls I throw.

I am lost in familiar body echoes—the burn
In the left palm, the pull in the right arm.

His eyes turn to brown legs and hips and breasts.
But I am ten and blazing in Candlestick Park,

Where I will again rewrite history and save
Game Seven of the '62 Series for my Giants.

I am firing the relay from center field to home,
And I die in the greatest throw ever made.

But my father's head is turning, turning
To a song, to a wave, to a bikini smile.

I hit his nose. His sunglasses wing away
Like a gull but land unbroken. *Jesus friggin'*

*Christ, kid! Give your old man a break, huh?*
*You need to learn to enjoy the . . . the sunshine . . .*

He chucks the next one that much harder,
And for a second, I feel my hand shatter.

A dark goddess in a white one-piece suit
Sighs, *Keep your eye on that ball, honey.*

He nods, returns to me, and smiles—
*Like this*, and he tosses one so softly

It lands silent in the aching glove.

Home Run, MacArthur Stadium, Syracuse, New York
*-for Jim Daniels-*

Somewhere in the cheap seats of left field,
My father cracked peanuts, drank Miller,
And hoped we were settled at last:
Four kids, four dogs, four Cokes.

The great wall of his patience collapsed
A kernel at a time onto the shoulders
Of the Syracuse Chief fans in front of us.

But between our squirming, our fighting,
And our begging for more food,
There came his salvation: that deep crack of the bat,
That baritone of connection with all things,
That possibility shooting him up into the ball's flight.

Standing, he cried, *Could be! Could be! Could be!*
And turned to draft beer hope
That the distant dot would clear the P&C sign,
Clear every failure and shortcoming,
Clear it all and disappear behind the stacked lights,
Where we, too, could lose ourselves
In one last exhalation of awe
Before we sat back down
To Cokes and dogs and Cracker Jacks falling.

*Lowering the Body*

## A White Baldness

The only time I ever saw
My proud, strident, reserved mother
Run like a schoolgirl toward my father
Was the night he lumbered up the porch
And peeled open the screen door
With his left hand, the right bandaged
And dangling—a white baldness.

He'd been making sausage,
Filling Labor Day orders.
He was alone, tired,
And the world bore down on him
Its ignorant metallic
Teeth, taking one fingertip
And then pieces, pieces.

She threw her arms around him.
She wept into his shoulders,
Shaking for work and hours and hope and money
And flesh and bone and worry and death.

And then she caught her breath
And returned to the music
Of the boiling rigatoni

As it filled the house.

## The Confetti

Uncle Mickey started working 60 hours a week
After my Cousin Peter shipped out for Vietnam.
Mickey sweated over wall-to-wall and linoleum,
Measuring and cutting mostly alone, never replacing
Peter: This was Mickey's war against the world
With his thick hands and battered Chevy Fleetside.

Mom made him take me to a football game,
Saying, *You gotta get back out into the world, Mick.*
He winced but agreed, the Utica Club in his hand
Becoming how I understood his hammers and nails,
His labored ascensions up staircases. I heard
Shoulder pain in the first glorious tall-neck swig.

This was a man whose boy would soon die,
His body blown down the Mekong River.
This was the fall of 1966, and not a time
For blue and white high-school cheerleaders
Crying because I stole two bags of their confetti
And tore them open down the chalked sideline.

So when two of them tackled me to the ground,
Mickey blew: *Kick those bitches to hell and back!*
But then his voice shook, *Leave him alone!*
*He's just a boy! He's only a kid! He's my son!*
His friends froze, holding him in their eyes
As the crowd burst into cheers over a first down.

Stunned, I was sorry for every snowing shred.

Aunt Dee

I

Deep in her mahogany cabinet,
In the black-and-white glossy I loved,
She glittered like ice on a Coke bottle:
She was third from the left, third,
High-stepping on the Radio City stage.
I wished the photo through a minefield
Of tea cups and put it back just before
She came in with the rest of that year's garlic.

In 1948, a Greyhound headed for Syracuse
Jumped the curb at 40$^{th}$ Street and clipped
Her so fast that the spike of her high heel
Stuck in the crack of the pavement,
And Dee flew ten feet. Her hip never recovered.

Still, my father clung to her story like I did:
She was the one who made it out: *She was a Rockette!*
He said it trimming pork chops for Mrs. Grimaldi.
He said it loading Curtis milk bottles into the coolers.
He said it weighing up fanning slices of corned beef or capicola.
He said it, said it, sang it in string,
Butcher paper, and sawdust—

He said it to everyone, everyone except Aunt Dee.

*Lowering the Body*

II

*Wars kill floors every time,* Mickey snapped
Open another can of Carling Black Label
And threw the old one to the floor of the truck.
We blurred through the burnt-orange October streets.
His store was failing, Peter was officially MIA,
And, over the phone, Mick fought with Dee all day.
Now, he flung us to Scriba to finish it in person.

On the front porch, she stood squinting at him,
Her hands never still in the apron:
*Don't bitch to me about life, Dee!*
*You run the store. You deal with the bank.*
*You talk to those Rochester supplier fucks, too!*
*If you weren't in those shittin' high heels,*
*None of this crap would've ever happened!*

Her face torched with my father's
Sicilian rage: *Then kiss my fat ass, Soldier Joe!*
Even I understood the depth of that cut.

Mickey tore through the flying stones of Phoenix Road
And would come home four days later with a black eye.
But we sat outside to ham, sweet potatoes, and baked beans.
Whispering grace, she touched my hand, and I thought,
*The foot tapping that empty chair has danced in front of the world.*

The sun set into the blood of the sky,
And she smiled as she cut the bread she baked for supper.

## Burying Cousin Peter

I

A month after we lowered Cousin Peter's body
Into July of 1967, the Ontario waves whispering
Below the cliffs at Saint Paul's Cemetery,
Uncle Mickey beat a man up onto his front porch
And out his side door, leaving him to bleed
Into the last green of that year's tomatoes.

This was Tommy Kyle, who swam
In Jim Beam that night at Romero's.
When Aunt Dee pulled her hand from his,
He said, *Who you kiddin', honey? You ain't
No Ziegfeld Follies girl, any more.* Mickey
Let it go, but Tommy mumbled it again
As they passed his house coming up Eighth.

*He was drunk with the rest of the stupids.
He took one look at her, so beautiful,
And he realized he was only born to die:*
With his chops, roasts, and steaks, my father
Weighed out his philosophies for days,

Mrs. Berlin smiling, listening, and nodding.

II

I was with Mickey in Peter's '53 Cadillac
When he parked it in Tommy Kyle's driveway—
A letter of apology, a key, and a closed door.

Then we crossed the street into beer and smoke and sauce.
Inside Romero's, I inhaled my life:
The weight of bowling-machine quarters an endowment,
My first beer, a Genny draft in a juice glass,
And Mickey already playing pinochle with the Delasio brothers,
Aunt Dee's birthday party as certain
As the box of Di Nobili cigars they opened.

And everybody showing up, knowing, trying
Not to look across Eighth Street
At the maroon emergence of Peter's Cadillac,
Its wraparound windshield hurling the sun.

And bowls and dishes and platters of sausage
And meatballs and cutlets and ziti and fettuccine.

And Mrs. Romero's fat arms tossing the *insalata*
With oil from Tuscany and vinegar from Modena.

And Grandpa Z's thick fingers giving the jukebox
The communion of coin after coin turning
Into Frank Sinatra, Louis Armstrong, and Herb Alpert.

Every last one of them fought for Mickey and Dee,
For the gift of the Caddy to Tommy Kyle,
For human sorrow, and the true letting go.

Mickey pulled back the curtain,
And they pretended not to notice, twirling their pasta harder,
Lifting brown bottles higher, living in stories a little longer.

And then the mandolin of the *tarantella*—faster and faster,
The circle grew to dark hands clapping
And arms becoming hearts rising.
And every word turned to music as Mickey looked one last time,
Saw the Caddy was gone, and lowered his head.

And they begged Aunt Dee onto the floor,
Where she spun and spun
On her good leg, then stood Mickey up and loved him
With olive eyes and a ring of calamari.

And Mrs. Romero freed her husband from the kitchen,
Twirling away day after day of his apron.
And they began the clockwise movement of this world
And then the counterclockwise answer to it.

And their feet were black shoes that blurred
Into my soul as even the strangers stood from their drinks,
Shouted their lives, and pounded their fists

Into the great oaken river of the wet black bar.

The Family Way

Grandma Z died, falling
Into her irises, marigolds, and petunias.
Her tomatoes had only begun
To leave their green,
Blushing pink like shy witnesses.

From across the county
They all rushed to Oswego Hospital—
Aunts, uncles, godparents,
Even prophetic Cousin Luigi,
Who had taken the week off work
To sip boilermakers down at Romero's,
Staring at the TV in black-and-white
Anticipation of impending doom.

This time, he was right.

Our family relished good news,
Savoring it like shrimp scampi at Christmas,
Delivering it in personal mouthfuls,
Sending ambassadors porch to porch.
They believed good news came from brown eyes
Smiling in your archway.
This was their way of stepping up to the inevitable,
Of raising their eyes to it,
And saying, *These, these ascensions are ours,
And you can never have them.*

But bad news was disseminated
In human electromagnetic panic,
Everyone staying close,
Shouldering a portion of the pull,
Shooing away what another couldn't.
They worked frantically,
Their eyes down,
Their hands never resting
To take a coat, get a drink,
Serve a plate of veal and peppers,
Or hold the head now fallen to grief.

Yes, they were tireless laborers,
Sweeping an onion field
Of every choking weed
Until the earth was black again,
Black and patient for the verdant pinstripes of green.

And so, my father closed the store,
The cousins all came in off the farms,
And like Dillinger's mob, we were off,
Absurdly driving the single block to the hospital.
You'd have thought it was the Kennedy assassination
All over again, the way they surrounded
Dr. Morgan, that poor cornered bastard,
Who kept insisting, *Please, please.*
*She died of a heart attack.*
*That's all we can say.*
*There isn't anything else to say.*

*I knew it. I knew it,* Luigi moaned.

No one questioned him.
Yet I saw in their faces
That no one believed in his vision, either.

But there could be no words about Luigi now:
To argue with him would be a standing still,
A yielding to death.

And there could be no stillness, either.
They shuffled or tapped their feet
On the thinning linoleum floor,
Pressing Dr. Morgan
Back against the wall,
Lurching at him
Like a bunch of Frankensteins.

Then something I'd never seen—
A moment of absolute quiet,
Just a tick or two of it,
As the doctor's face wore
Its final rational tolerance.

*Well, okay,* my father said, arms rising.
*It sounds like you did all you could, Doc.*

Even at eleven, I knew that it was not possible
For a man to look more incredulous
Than Dr. Morgan did at that moment.
After all, she was DOA.
The room ignited in jittery sobbing,
No staid harmony to their weeping,
Some of them saying something,
Any incomprehensible thing
Until, of one mind, they turned like a school of fish,
And there were plans and strategies
And meals to be cooked:
There was organization enough
To satisfy any counter-revolutionary.

The uncles led shaking Grandpa Z,
And we emerged as one lamenting song
From the shadows of the Emergency Tunnel,
Fanning out into the shimmering parking lot,
Where, heads bowed low,
We helped one another
Back into our Buicks, Pontiacs, and Oldsmobiles,

Two or three of which were still running.

## Lowering the Body

*. . . and still the door said nothing and slept.*

James Tate
"The Wrong Way Home"

Once upon a time,
On the corner of West Fourth and Oneida,
A boy was somehow locked
In a funeral home bathroom.

He was lost in brassy wonderment
To the roll call of the grieving,
And the door, older than creaking bone,
Slept on its hinges
And shut its keyhole eye.

Then the archway yawned him out
To stand among empty chairs
And peek from behind a curtain
As the director cranked the coffin,
Lowering the grandmother's body
Into the seal of the closing lid.

And in his collapse,
He fell with her into flowers,
The world piercing his heart
Into the doors of sleep
As he discovered the dark-carpeted
Weightlessness of death.

## Vittorio and Conchetina

He loved her with the purity
Of November snow blanketing
The black earth of his onion fields.

He loved her with the restlessness
Of a farmer harvesting the days—
All for her stove, her face, her hands.

He loved her with all of the grace
That came poured in her minestrone,
That sudden burst of Roma

Tomatoes in Sicilian eyes.

Your Knives
*-after Alicia Ostriker's "Cows"-*

The morning after Grandpa Z's funeral,
You rose older, heavier,
Made the familiar way
Around Eighth, and opened the store.
Imperceptibly slower
But slower still,
The key from the pocket,
Then selected in the hand,
Then turned in the lock,
And you flicked the lights
Into their humming.

In the last days
When folks thought he was crazy,
You had him behind the meat counter,
Your old teacher alive again
With a knife in his hand,
Trimming sirloin with mathematical precision,
Boning out pork butts for sausage,
Then cubing beef for hamburger,
His hands conducting the music
Of meat, blade, and bone bucket.

And one afternoon
You turned and saw him
Staring down at an old knife
Balanced in the palm of his hand.

He said, *You see? This isa beautiful.*
*They carve it just for you.*

You'd heard it before,
The beauty of the bottles,
Boxes, cans, and knives
Of our time.

Customers called for prosciutto,
Salami, and the sliced provolone.
But you watched the sun
Cover his thick hands.

*Okay, Pa,* you said, helping him
To his chair by the bread,
Where he told stories to the loaves.

But alone that morning,
You stood at your butcher block
And saw the line of knives.
And the world was perfect—
Each can, box, jar, or loaf
In its absolute place,
And each one a thing of beauty.

Knives.
Your Knives.
Your knives along the wall.
Your knives as they woke from sleep.
Your knives as they moved you from pain to hours
As you took the sharpest one down from the silver strip
And followed it blade and roast and string and story into the day.

Kahn the Great

Kahn had us leaning forward in our bleachers just about to tip—
Red pins, green pins, orange pins, blue pins:
He flung them miles above his head
As life spun on in sugared howls.

Then thunder hammered
Above the Family Fun Circus tent,
And pin after pin slammed down
On the Great Kahn's head.

His music jangled forward,
Lurching out the score for a changing universe.

His assistant, all curves in a red sequined suit,
Still stood there, arms outstretched, fingers
Insistent in their pointing celebration
Of his great juggling skill.

An explosion of children
Rose and inhaled the comedy of failure.

*You pricks! You little shits!*
*You laugh at Kahn the Great?*
*I played Barnum when I was five!*
*I juggled for FDR!*
*I was The Wizard Boy!*

Then the midget clowns surrounded him,
Holding his hands with their painted pity

As three roadies burst into the ring
To pick up the dozen pins

Just before The Princess Isabella cracked her whip
At the line of prancing white stallions
All glittering with golden manes
And erasing time to wild applause.

We sat down and sighed in popcorn-awe as she rode around the ring
And stood glowing on each successive horse.
In seconds, they surrounded her,
And perfect order was restored.

## My Mother Joins the Hippies

They came down from the hill of Oswego State again—
Frayed bell-bottoms, flowing hair, a river of tie-dyed
Acid colors, headbands, peace necklaces, granny sunglasses,
Beads, vests, boots, sandals, and braided leather belts that made
Them look like the Franciscans who taught us Sunday school.

The hippies turned south off Bridge and silently carried
Their signs on Eighth, moving past the store, emptied now
Of awe-struck customers who clung to their wrapped roasts,
Their quarts of milk, their pounds of olives, their loaves of bread,
Who clung to the corner of West Eighth and Oneida itself.

This time, it wasn't the latest LBJ troop surge in Vietnam
And the city hall sit-in with its chants of *Make Love, Not War!*
That produced "The Oswego Nine," still awaiting trial.
No. This time, the hippies protested because our own Mrs. Thompson
Down on Mohawk had been forced from her Second Grade classroom

At Leighton Elementary: She was three months pregnant and showing.
When the story broke in the neighborhood, it moved woman to woman,
Yard to yard like a swarm of angry bees, and my mother's
Dark Polish face hardened from beauty to political outrage.
*Politics is bad for business. Stay out of it!* my father yelled

Into the wall behind the meat counter. Those aisles kept them from killing
Each other when they disagreed. They waited until it was only us kids:
He was in the produce aisle pretending to straighten heads of lettuce,
And she was in the canned-goods aisle pretending to block the shelves.
They shouted to each other things they could never discuss at home:

His arguments rounded displays of Del Monte peaches;
Her retorts bounced off boxes of Kellogg's Corn Flakes;
And the air inside the store was somehow the final arbiter.
They taught us fair exchange, one finally turning silent, nodding,
Picking up a broom, and sweeping forward for us all.

But that time, at her check-out counter, she ignored him by stocking
Nestlé bars, Teaberry gum, and Marlboros while insisting
To customers, *Right is right, wrong is wrong, and there's nothing wrong
With a pregnant woman teaching Second Grade.* Then she whipped
That rotary dial phone until she stood informing our principal,

*Well then, shop elsewhere for your liverwurst and Monks' bread!*
It took months for my father to learn she had banned Dr. Burlunder,
But it only took seconds for her to cross Eighth Street in her uniform,
Carrying the grocery stamper higher and higher like some kind of baton.
Mrs. Berlin, Mrs. Ferraro, and Mrs. Grimaldi joined the hippies, too.

They shook hands, talked, and nodded, no one looking a bit out of place.
They would chant all the way to Dr. Burlunder's house on Sixth and Utica.
Customers looked to my father to do something but then ambled home.
He shrugged his shoulders, ushered us inside, closed the store for the day,
Went behind the meat counter, and cut down a hanging provolone.

He nodded as he carved away the wax, kept on nodding as he sliced Genoa,
Tore bread, poured olives, and opened up bottles of pop and Genesee.
Stretching on the sawdust, he addressed the remaining two cheeses:
*This one talks but says nothing. This one says nothing but knows everything.*
My brother Mike wanted to know, *So how come they get along?*

*Go figure,* he said. *Maybe it's a bigger window than they know.*
Of course, we had no idea what the hell he was talking about:
We just giggled as his story grew with the voices of knives, saws, and scales.
His hands opened, and he looked like Grampa Z so much that I ached,
But only until the sharp cheese and rich olives filled the air,

And the first sweet burn of the Coke swept it all away.

## My Mother's Goose-Stepping Rage

*Darts like hot coals went through my legs
and arms and I howled more loudly still. And
then, just when I was sure I was finished, a
shriek ten times as loud as mine came blaring
off the cliff. It was my mother! She came roaring
like thunder, screaming like a thousand hurricanes,
eyes as bright as dragonfire . . .*

    John Gardner
    *Grendel*

### I

Pockets stuffed with Nestlé bars and Sugar Daddies,
We blazed our way toward the Oswego Theatre

For John Wayne's heroics in *The Green Berets*.
But what good was a boy during a war movie

Without the proper caramel-and-chocolate
Ball to work his jaws to exhaustion in the dark?

I had forgotten my Milk Duds, so I dragged my brother
Into Boscov's store. We were warned they were nuts,

Hiding behind their curtain, leaving you to stand among
Dead shelves until dusty Wheaties' athletes stared

Back. Mrs. Boscov flew from the curtain's design,
An eagle-nosed, weed-headed woman, eyes

Scowling at her candy counter and then at me.
She wrapped both hands around my elbow.

Her son's brilliant Chopin brought tears to our eyes
Year's later. But now, my brother burned for home,

And I sank into the moor of her accusation.
I could not explain the opened box of Dots

Or the Milky Way or the M&M's bulging in my pockets.

II

Outside, she was a wind of vicious Russian,
And I saw the back of her head open up

To the vast Oswego blueness over us.
She kicked me, demanding the candy

That she didn't even sell. *And then, just when
I was sure I was finished* . . . there came

A roaring Polish from up on Sixth Street,
Where my mother goose-stepped the horizon.

Part of me loved this international showdown,
The Russian weed woman against the pissed Polish mother

Who kicked the bully back behind her curtain. Oh, years
Later, Georgie Boscov would die driving back to Cornell,

And I would pray for his soul to ascend like whole notes.
But on that afternoon, everything melting in my pockets,

What did I know but joy and fear, the world ground
Down to a halt, my mother walking us back home

Through the very vapor trail she had left when she
Howled like Ontario thunder, breaking over the hill,

Her enraged love searing its way down Oneida Street.

In Love with the B-Girls

I wanted the girl left at the bar just before
John Wayne and Susan Hayward lit up
Their cigarettes in *The Fighting Seabees*.

Again, Uncle Joe took us to the Saturday matinee,
Got us in for a buck, and said, *That John Wayne
Shoulda ran for president*. My brothers nodded,

But I was mystified that the camera never returned to her,
Or never returned to the dark beauty leaving the hotel
Behind Robert Mitchum in *Cape Fear*, or never returned

To the woman who shook behind Elvis in *Viva Las Vegas*.
Where did they go when they left those clubs, or shot
Through those crossfire lobbies, or danced off the screen

Of another world while my neck strained around corners?
One by one, they arrived on cue across my bedroom ceiling
To float above the stories of mere actors and actresses:

Oh, my B-girls drank away the sorrows of this world,
Narrowly escaped their flesh-and-blood torments,
Danced themselves free from life's B-love affairs,

And lived in the celluloid behind my closed eyes.

Blessings, Cursings: The Chained Shelves

**I: The Dismantling**

And the slab of the checkout counter with its oaken
Rivers worn in ancient grain, and the tilted shelves
Of penny candy and cigarettes, all empty behind it?
    Keep, keep, oh, God,
    Keep it all nailed to the floor,
    Forever a bridge of hands,
    Bread, olives, soup, change, smiles,
    And sliced ham wrapped in white paper

Keep them keep them keep them all

And the aisles refusing to dull in darkness,
This endless counting of tile after tile
Into the lives that wore each step before me?
    Down, oh, up and down them all
    Into lives once and always
    Wish them to the pathways
    Between West Eighth and Oneida
    And the worlds behind front doors

Wish them wish them wish them all

## II: Movers with Cigarettes

And the bare walls, exposed slats,
A disease to the touch, and this sliver under
The thumbnail of *Shit, shit, shit* echoing?
    Open, open, open like a wound
    For what's beyond this place,
    And damn the eyes of accusers
    Frozen open in knots of wood,
    Their faces in every inch of these walls

Damn the distances we now must go

And the movers grunting with Winstons dangling
Ashes to black boots with Cokes and dirty jokes,
And our shelving screaming then chained to a flatbed Ford?
    Curse, curse, curse them all
    With the tarot of my baseball cards,
    My best Mickey Mantle rubbed in hatred
    As those thieves back into our door
    And are gone to grinding gears up Eighth,

Where I run after, the *fuck-you's* bursting inside my lungs

And overhead, an abacus of blackbirds falls from the wires

# Coda: Saby Closes the Store, January, 1969

## Saby Closes the Store, January, 1969
*-for my parents-*

There had to be a final customer,
One last, *Sold American!* from him,
All smiles, as anyone would remember.
Maybe Casper across the street stopped in
To shoot the breeze and find out for himself
If what he heard down at the Elk's was true.
Or Mrs. D picked Campbell's from the shelf,
And he tossed in a box of Saltines, too.
I'd like to think it could've been his wife
Taking Juicy Fruit and flipping him a dime,
That they talked more about their love than their strife,
And that they thanked each other for the time.
I'd like to think that he wasn't alone
When he locked up, rounded Eighth, and came home.

*The photo above on the left shows Stephen, in 1963, "helping" in his parents' grocery store.*

STEPHEN MURABITO is Professor of English at the University of Pittsburgh's Greensburg campus. His short stories have appeared in such places as *North American Review*, *Antietam Review*, *Sou'wester*, *Brooklyn Review*, and *Paper Street*. He has been an NEA Fellow in Poetry, and his poems have appeared in such places as *Minnesota Review*, *Mississippi Review*, *Poet Lore*, and *5AM*. His chapbook, *A Little Dinner Music*, was published by Parallel Press in 2004. The first book of his Oswego trilogy, *The Oswego Fugues*, came out from Star Cloud Press in 2005; the second book of his Oswego trilogy, *Communion of Asiago*, came out from Star Cloud Press in 2006. His poems are anthologized in *Encore: More of Parallel Press Poets* (Parallel Press, 2006); *Joyful Noise: An Anthology of American Spiritual Poetry* (Autumn House Press, 2006); and *Along These Rivers* (Quadrant Publishing, 2008). He is also the author and editor of the composition textbook *Connections, Contexts, and Possibilities* (Prentice Hall, 2001). He lives in Saltsburg, Pennsylvania, with his wife, April, and their four children Angie, Stella, Toni, and Sebastian.

Stephen Murabito's *The Oswego Fugues* is a brilliant, ambitious book, the work of a mature, confident poet. Stylistically rich and varied, this beautiful poem is full of tender memories juxtaposed against the hard edges of hard lives. This is a work of deep faith and imagination. Of faith in the imagination. Of a poet trying to preserve Oswego, a place he loves, and the people who live and die there. These meditations on memory and loss often turn into soaring incantatory flights of lyric passion, elegiac and sweet."—-Jim Daniels, Author of *Show and Tell: New and Selected Poems*, University of Wisconsin Press

ISBN: 1-932842-04-7

Publisher: Star Cloud Press,
Year of Publication: 2005, $ 22.95
Format: paperback, 7 ½ x 9 ¼,
page count: 143

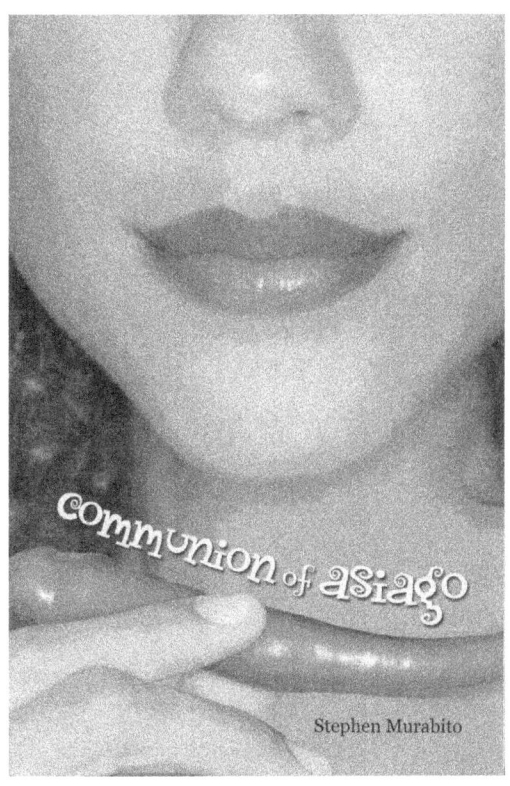

Food and family and music are the central figures in Stephen Murabito's wonderful *Communion of Asiago*, a book whose broad humor and warm storytelling invite the reader to "taste, hear, and see." Whether invoking the ordinary pleasures of bread and cheese, sausage and beer; or the more exotic charms of artichokes and garlic, Beaujolais and escargot; these poems reveal how "the simple will become magic." In his easy, affectionate voice, Murabito praises the sensory, from his family's homemade kielbasa and kiszka, to Sonny Rollins's "last goosehonk toot." For Murabito, food is the music of love—and of peace, forgiveness, grace, and mercy—urging us all not to "be strange anymore," but to "defy death and sing." *Communion of Asiago* will tickle anyone's palate, satisfy anyone's hunger; it's a real symphony, a feast. —Ronald Wallace, Author of *Long for This World* (University of Pittsburgh Press)

Star Cloud Press, 73 pages, $ 14.95

*Communion of Asiago* by Stephen Murabito

www.ingramcontent.com/pod-product-compliance
Lightning Source LLC
Chambersburg PA
CBHW030004050426
42451CB00006B/115